A SKY OF LATE SUMMER

A SKY

OF

LATE SUMMER

❧ POEMS ❧

By

HENRY RAGO

THE UNIVERSITY OF CHICAGO PRESS

CHICAGO AND LONDON

Standard Book Number: 226-70309-6
Library of Congress Catalog Card Number: 78-92464
The University of Chicago Press, Chicago 60637
The University of Chicago Press, Ltd., London

FOR JULIET
ANEW

ACKNOWLEDGMENTS

"The Coming of Dusk Upon a Village in Haiti" and "The Painting Lesson," in somewhat different form as "Childhood Painting Lesson," appeared originally in *The New Yorker*.

"A Church in the Martinique" was first published in *Chicago Review*.

"My Mother's Portrait," under the title "A Painting," and "The News of Winter," in an earlier, longer version, were published in *The Quarterly Review of Literature*.

"A Child's Birthday" was published first as "A Birthday" in *The Sewanee Review*. This poem too has been considerably revised.

"Morning Above Port-au-Prince" and "A Map Kept as a Souvenir" appeared originally in *The Hudson Review*.

The following poems have been published in *Poetry*: "The Net," "The Knowledge of Light," "Poem for an Anniversary," "The Quarrel," "Departures," "Promise Your Hand," "The Temple," "The Summer Countries," "How the Bright Earth Spun Like a Jewel" (1 through 4), "The House" (including "Sit Now, Quietly"), "Presence of Statues," "The Attending," "The Distances," "A Sky of Late Summer," "The Promising," "Unchristened Time Came Ignorant to That Day" and "The Green Afternoon" (published as "Two Poems"), and seven "Inscriptions" ("The Remembrance of a Young Girl Sketching the Children of Positano," "The News of Winter," "The Lovers," "For a Dead Actress," "The Presence," "The Snapshot," and "The Letter: Morning").

The Trilogy that is Part I—"A Sky of Late Summer," "The Knowledge of Light," "The Attending"—was published in Italy in 1959 by Palmaverde (Bologna) as a separate volume under the title *Conoscenza della Luce*, a bilingual edition with the Italian versions by Alfredo Rizzardi.

"Praise of Comedy: A Discourse" was published in somewhat different form as a chapbook in 1963 by The King and Queen Press, Williamsburg.

"In That Fierce Country" and "Provence: Three Marriage Songs" were first published in *Botteghe Oscure*.

Much work with this book and the finding of its true shape were made possible by a year's leave in Europe, 1960–61, for which the author acknowledges a permanent debt to the Rockefeller Foundation.

CONTENTS

I
Triptych

II
Cities, Islands

III
The House: A Cycle of Poems

IV

Presences

A SKY OF LATE SUMMER

I

Triptych

A SKY OF LATE SUMMER

I

The fountains of fire
Play in the deep sky
Their wild becoming,
Spray upon spray.

Will the fountains of August
Be held by the names
Of a child's beasts
In the glistering cage?

By secret numbers
Drawn from the fire?
But how the night trembles
Star upon star!

So the wild light
Arches and falls
And the fountains of language
Arch, fall,

Until stirred with no word
The deep heart
Far beneath its own fountain
Unspent though spent far

Lifts with a cry
To the heart of that fire
And cries no name
But is named in the pure

Flaming that utters
The visible flame,
Breath of all naming,
Speech of each name:

Is! Is!
Bursting to spell
The words and the names
In the blessing spilled

Star after star,
Spray upon spray:
The deep midnight's
Perpetual day.

II

The legend *Est* to be marked on the door of the inn
Where the wine was good, on the one door
The servant's writing tripled to music:
Est, Est, Est! to name that wine
Deep in its being, vintage
Of the long becoming, and the stirring of the earth
Trembling to turn, and turning
Trembling in the bed of summer for the great
Shaft of the sun. O warm becoming
In the coming of the green-silver
Half-sun, half-earth: and the grape
Secret with light and dark, a season of
Midnights and mornings rolled round, green-silver—
A continent gathered.
                              It is! It is!
This glass of light, light to be
Touched. Light
Spoken to the tongue. Clear moment of being
For the dark tangled history, this

One simpleness, one fluent crystal, raised
For the sprawling roots, for the torn calendar.

III

This way, made by this way, to make
The point at the center, to hold fast
North, South, the East by West,
And all things drawn by four winds, withdrawn
Now from their names, and named to be drawn
In the one sign: this is to part
The seas for their whispered name, to cry
The torrents of change and their thronging names
Beyond unsaying: Ens
Realissimus, being clear Being,

The world's shattered heart.

IV

As if on all the strings of poetry,
Each poem a string—

        As if
The iridescent world, layer beneath
Diaphanous layer—

        As if within
The essences of Grasse, the keen, clean
Breath of the Alps—

        Or fugitive between
The finger-tip and the drift of hair—

O poured like wine! Given—
The vast clear Given—

V

Tumbled into circuses of stars,
Spun to the silk of light or the blown
Air, this Plenitude
Smiles through my sciences. O exquisite
It balances on a finger-tip the *is*
Of logic, or holds all mathematics weighed
On the thin equal-sign where the equations
Cross and re-cross
That could be set to spinning in a star.

Leaping in words and words
It keeps no grammar where the words
Are one pure silver. No subject stammers
To find the hazard of its predicate.
Lo, the first and long
Last fluency, the free breath,
Lyric of lyric, joy rejoicing:
Song.

THE KNOWLEDGE OF LIGHT

I

The willow shining
From the quick rain,
Leaf, cloud, early star
Are shaken light in this water:
The tremolo of their brightness: light
Sung back in light.

II

The deep shines with the deep.
A deeper sky utters the sky.
These words waver
Between sky and sky.

III

A tree laced of many rivers
Flows into a wide slow darkness
And below the darkness, flowers again
To many rivers, that are a tree.

IV

Wrung from silence
Sung in lightning
From stone sprung

The quickening signs
Lines quivered
Numbers flew

Darkness beheld
Darkness and told
Each in each
The depths not darkness.

V

To know
Meaning to celebrate:
Meaning
To become "in some way"
Another; to come
To a becoming:
To have come well.

VI

Earth wakens to the word it wakens.

These dancers turn half-dreaming
Each to the other, glide
Each from a pool of light on either side
Below the dark wings
And flutter slowly, come slowly
Or drift farther again,
Turn to the single note, lifted,
And leap, their whirling lines
Astonished into one lucidity:
Multiples of the arc.

Shapes of the heart!

The year waits at the depth of summer.
The air, the island, and the water
Are drawn to evening. The long month
Is lost in the long evening.

If words could hold this world
They would bend themselves to one
Transparency; if this
Depth of the year, arch of the hour
Came perfect to
The curving of one word
The sound would widen, quietly as from crystal,
Sphere into sphere: candor
Answering a child's candor
Beyond the child's question.

THE ATTENDING

I

The Sunday endless on the wide bank,
The mill silent, the children
Half-sunlight in the spill and fall of white
Gold; a skill of blue-white,
Green-white, violet, where
They stand in shallows,
The burst to faint fire
Where they have leapt;
And where they stand or move,
These delicate shafts of light in light
Poised, trembling:
This grave dance
Attending.

II

From grey landscape, from the dusty web of roads
The roads turn, have turned
To the good village on the good day
Or the valley immediate in sunlight
Where we said
It was a good place, stayed
And were happy. We remembered later
How—but not quite how—the earth
Came to a brightening!
The year of our first child's coming
We traced, white on the grey of February,

10

The first pale almond-blossoms
From village to village, northward
Slowly to Rome,
And the gentle leap of that brush
Through Umbria, over
The earth-shapes, earth-colors, until
Suddenly at Assisi, it was
All of Assisi!
                    Gathered upon the hill,
A grace met with grace,
Well met,
Where it was good for us to be.

III

The words have shone and rippled and run like leaves
Or have risen like waves, sloped and broken
Endlessly, countlessly, counting one music
That waits there always,
As coming again after months or years
The car grinds over the last turn
On the last hill
And we find again or are found by
The unchanged music, keeping
That moment and the long day,
The hours of sleep and the vast promise
Spread bright from the awakening.
The words are
Broken on the poem as the waves are broken,
As the poem at last is broken
On a farther music
And poem after poem—how many!—
Broken.
                    For these words' rising
And for the deep guess of their breaking

11

The hours and years
Slide huge,
Shapeless, nameless, to the poise
Of hazard crossed on hazard
And signed in the moment's
Luck of light,
Luck; by the thanks for it.

IV

Not in the sea but in this that changes the sea
And greets the Franciscan hill and hovers
On the dazed river and the slope and the delicate bathers;
In the breath shaping the song, in the motion between
The heart's motion and the pulsing world
Attend:
    we are attended
And we attend. O courteous light
That holds these courtesies! Arches of thin fire
Leap with this swift love;
Ardors of air, alleluias of sun
Sing marriage!

Fame of this day:
Earth's fame;
Ours.

II

Cities, Islands

IN THAT FIERCE COUNTRY

In that fierce country, not Ophelia's lap,
Speech burns to verse, the play within a play
Consumes the play and all the world, nor stops
To hear the king demand, "What means this play?"
The arch dissolves, the immense chorus slopes
Downward to mist and dark, upward from tribes
To chosen tribe, to prophet, to the dim shapes
Of the one shape twisted into a cry.

In that fierce country which is no one's love,
Life burns to love, the play beyond the play
Turns self to not-self, and the audience moves
In pageant to the slow rise of the play
As victim becomes priest. The wide earth heaves
To rock, to temple, to the single height
Where all art trembles to lyric and forgives
All art. There is no curtain but the light.

THE COMING OF DUSK UPON A VILLAGE IN HAITI

The island that had flowered to the sun
Folded the night into its dark hills. Slow
Gestures of wind signed over it with sleep.
A dust of silver weighed upon the leaves
And touched the village roofs half into air.

Soft, soft, the air insisted: all things now
Be muted to the night, be drugged, be dumb,
Like that brown girl and boy who gravely move
Sleepwalking toward each other; like these leaves
Huge in a dream, luxurious with fatigue.

And darkness subtle as an undersea
Became the secret touch upon the ferns,
Smothered the burning poinciana, quenched
All but the deepest red. All that could live
Lived only in one swollen influence.

O from that sea of jasmine, where no word
Could find its breath, and tambours from the hills
Spoke to the night, the helpless mind turned still
Its pale look upward; and the heart, that last
Bloom of conspiracy, would not be lost!

A CHURCH IN THE MARTINIQUE

Neither the Place des Vosges pure and exact
As those clear laws that gracefully detained
Monsters in wigs of stone guarding the steps
Of some new bagatelle to please whatever
Mistress or cardinal, and poised the strict
Essays upon the quiet Loire to keep
River and light and distance circumspect

Nor this outburst of earth, shapeless as thatch,
Amorous of the strangely vapored night,
Artless with huge blossoms and clumsy leaves,
Its children naked and its dark girls fetched
Like mangoes in the bush—candor that hides
Its own lie, calling rum to charm the blood
To this strange sun, the mind to a child's French—

But wretched Saint Pierre, a slice of board,
Adoring for his Queen the tinseled doll,
And this dark hole, the blacks down from the hills
Waiting to lisp their sins: they stole or lied
Or rubbed a charm. You come the last of all.
This is the needle's eye. Your treacherous guide
The two-faced fury smiles to see you crawl.

THE QUARREL

So the years argue, the murderous voices
Shout our treasons. Once more we shiver
Before the shrill account; always the same
Sure light to scatter us; poor wreckage of clothes,
The cold mirror. Walls mocking the lovers.

So the years snarl our astounding names,
Jaws baffled by no country. Ah, they
Have leapt at every window, they will have us
Over and over, though we change
A hundred houses and a hundred rooms.

What word that is no word will charm
The huge assassins? The air with treble tongues
Cries with our breath, assumes our faces
Crazy in a film. Our selves are plunged
To that compelling league we cannot name.

And only unbelief can stand against
The visit. This hand, hideous and lame,
A world from yours, is unreal where it lies.
Beneath their mad alarm, my eyes, your eyes,
Strain through the scourge for one last innocence.

PRESENCE OF STATUES

They were always there, for our returning
Across the Seine, or for the ponderous
Returning of the city from the night
To the vast dull silver blurred with the Tuileries,
The Louvre, or just so much of it, and the sky's
Quiet awareness. There, as the forms and lines
Slowly composed themselves within the grey
Etching, they stood, the heads massive, impassive,
The eyes closed, as if
The heads had never turned, and merest stone
Disowned all plot or portent:
See, nothing has moved, the stage is empty.

And scenes and seasons played out on that stage
Brilliant or dim before those cold
Witnesses, still rage of boredom,
To whom the play always returned; watchers
Above the uncertain trail from one late *tabac*'s
Closing to another's darkening down
Until the last pale neon wavered alone
In the enormous dawn that would disclose
Paris, and those eyelids of stone on stone.

MORNING ABOVE PORT-AU-PRINCE

The sun spreads like a drum-beat in the East
As Ti-Pau swings his wagon into the yard
And scatters the wretched hens in a storm of feathers,
The horse's head and the banana leaves
Shaking like doom over the foolish beasts.

He has no shoes, this Ti-Pau, and no father,
But a handsome day's afloat, and not the least
Abject or brash he sings to his tall God.
"Bon jour," he sings over the small stampede,
"Bon jour" to the noble sky, "Bon jour, Ministre."

MY MOTHER'S PORTRAIT

Your world is under glass. What storms I can re-
      member now
Are faëry. My own child's-voice is muted
As in a far world on a dim music floated
I hear it speak to you.

I have been away, and now I sit again where your
      eyes command
The world of their peace, not asking or telling
Of any season but the one beyond failing
Enclosed forever in your hands.

It rains. I am troubled. And I beg as I have always
      done,
Stranger to stranger, always across the thousand
Fears of the night and in all my world's strange
      houses,
Pray for your son.

DEPARTURES

End of summer; the waiter
Shrugging when I ask for more than
The note says. Last pull of the
Taut nerve at the abandoned café.
The sun is a cold fire on the siphon bottle;
The rust comes through the green paint.

End of summer; the concierge
Not so friendly now when I press for more
Exact intelligence. "Greece? But where?
With whom? with that one?"
The dog in the corner opens one eye,
And the shabby guest stirs her coffee.

Ah, there are wheels that could crush this city,
Grinding down every mistake, murdering the voices
That would prevent. There is a station that invites
    me
Into its perpetual half-light.

End the summer. A vessel
Is patient in harbor, promising eastward,
One more stage eastward—
As we lunge again like lovers, like children again hope
For the place where the legend will be real as birds
And olive leaves hang marvelous with sleep.

III

The House
A Cycle of Poems

PROMISE YOUR HAND

Promise your hand. Slow, slow, the dawn
And I am spun through ten years'
Seas and cities. Uncertain trees
Pursue the road; and though I take
The next train, draw the shade,
Names not in my language
Beat at the window, cold enemies
Sit opposite, masked
In the local headlines, their wine and bread
Not for my asking. They
Lurch and wind among the dark
Mountains. I am searched at the frontier,
Walled in grey uniforms, I am flung
To the high unwanted room to count
My foreign coins like minutes, with the bent
Concierge watching from the hall
Wishing me neither good nor harm
Wishing me nothing. Look, the vague trees
Clutch even here, now not so tall
But clutching. Promise your hand,
I will speed these rails again, leap
By these lights, hide between cars,
But be, only be the patient and sure
Miracle of yourself at the last far station,
Implausible point on the wild map
Suddenly real and from what great arc
Marvelously catching my flight; containing me.

THE TEMPLE

A legend of Paestum

Locusts, the ragged crows, the water grass,
The snakes. All these were as the map had warned
The engineer at home in Mantua.
He left his swans for this malarial
Sty. The gain would be a road, no more.
So there were flies and fever, as each day
Tore something from the sweating trees, and light
Wormed through the black growth. But nothing
    provided
That one day Piero, straining ahead
Of his strange men and their dark dialect
Should see beyond the thicknesses of black,
Above the swamp's delirium, that clarity
Of hard Greek suddenly and always there
And waiting: Poseidonia! Poseidonia!
O for that pure cool utterance of columns
Into Corinthian blossoms, for that pale
City beyond all breath, the debased language
Lay dumb as lizards on the temple steps,
The fierce sun waited upon pink and gold
And white, and the barbarous trees parted.

THE HOUSE

This love would be a prodigy. It cries
Within its trembling moment to avow
More than itself. It will not be
What may or may not be; it makes to be.
It is no statement but a vow.

This love would be a shining enterprise:
Shaped by geometry of hands, it makes
A house of air; it is its lord
And tenant, its deed is its simple word.
It is the gradual house it makes.

And as its law is love, its grammar is
No grammar and no logic, but the love
Which is the rhetoric of itself
In promise and fulfillment of itself.
Love is the prodigy of love.

THE SUMMER COUNTRIES

Opened, clear as a child's geography,
The summer countries, the hills
Folding and unfolding. Sunlight
Stretched long upon the beach, hung
Folded and unfolded in the nets:
The land a long morning, the morning
A land, its hours clear and still
As pebbles, corals, blue shells.

As for the first time opened

And the whole sky caught among
Its nets and pebbles, the country never
And always open, and time burst
Into the first time, fell
Cadenzas of first light along
The long beach. It was
Both land and morning, and the light
Was loud and everywhere, like bells.

HOW THE BRIGHT EARTH SPUN LIKE A JEWEL

1

How the bright earth spun like a jewel,
Like a wizard's toy, like the first of three wishes,
And whirled and blurred until its lights were all
And all its colors all
And we from large in nothing fell
To small in all,
And the gradual nothing to suddenly all
And all before us, let the smallest
Song tell,
Spinning as simply as its simple
Syllable
And over and over and
Over, for it is
All.

2

And found ourselves in a blue country,
The people friendly, the inns
Decent and cool. White lace was lavished
On a great bed, there was a clock
Little and brave and earnest,
The family's good curtains, sun on the floor,
The earth outside like a good beast,
And all else curving blue, blue, bluest
In such a sky we wept, oh such a sky!

3

Or it was a play then, danced
As your eyes danced,
And the scene of the carnival glittered
As your eyes glittered.
The wounded lived
If you turned toward them with pity
Once; and if you smiled once
The ogre was confounded and they led him away
To everyone's tittering.

The music was commanded
As you moved your hand.

And it was your applause that availed
The play's ending,
Touching the enchanted
With the extraordinary real
And dissolving the
Delicate prison of lights
In light.

4

See, see our cities, how the domes
Float in the sun, now the towers
March on every hill, no sea
But kneels before these harbors.
See the bridges thrown
Slender as light or strong
As armies. A thousand streets
Weave the delicate map.
                                        See

From this hill, this bridge, this sea,
The cities rising to their names.
We speak the names, and the
Domes float, the towers
March.
                    Empire
Wide as our joy! Let these names
Claim the hills and hold
The obedient sea. Let the sky
Bend—

5

Now our three colors splash upon the air,
Leap the old towers, trumpet with the sun;
The city from a sleep long as the Seine
Astonishes the day: the squads of hours
Wheel and unroll down the green avenues
Loud with our flag, bright with our Marseillaise.

THE GREEN AFTERNOON

Translucent green on the wall, a dance of leaves,
  Of hands weaving
Peace like a vine on the bedroom wall,

And the white gauze curtains blown
  Of wind or light
Suspend the green afternoon

As the room suspends
  And is the whole house, is the day
Or the one clarity of the day

Asserting its clear furniture,
  Confirming
The definition of itself

Like a choice
  Returned to and returned to, like
A luminous choice.

PROVENCE: THREE MARRIAGE SONGS

1. *Wine*

The bridal summer flows
Gold as Cassis by day,
And there is darker wine
That does not need the day
But deeply knows
The depth, the depth of day.

2. *The Bicycles*

Sun in the wheels, and the wheels singing.
Is it the sun the wheels are singing?
It is the sun that spins! The sun singing!

3. *The Garland*

Orange and Avignon and Arles
That twist the garland of the Rhône,
Diana's colony is gone,
Her city lies beneath
The Holy Marys of the Sea:
Your fame this living afternoon
Is this one girl, my bride, who wears
Your garland in the sun;
And the Holy Marys of the Sea
Whose Grace she bears.

Unchristened time came ignorant to that day.
Graceless it fell to grace, saltless it was
Preserved for salt. Its untold days told as
One daybreak for a calendar of days,
Sun to its anniversaries. So time
Comes to its time, as nameless once it came
Upon the softest mention of its name.

SIT NOW, QUIETLY

Sit now, quietly, while the last
Phantoms diminish and dissolve, and the
Lost voices droop upon their argument.
Your silence will forgive all argument,
The sanctuary of your hands hold fast
The real from unreal, hold the free.

Look now, openly, with the clear
Courtesy of your eyes: a closure draws
Its peace upon the compass of your sight.
O when at last you sleep, I beg you close
In your closed eyes my world, and safely bear
The world to morning within your good night.

IV

Presences

THE NET

For my students at the University of Chicago, 1947–1954

A wide net I needed
When that room leapt with words
Here to the left, and there
Where I almost missed. Or the words
Were all the net there was:
The walls
Faded, the room
Lithe as a net
Stirred, a wide low
Shimmering. It was
Such poor thread as we had,
Tied upon thread:
Speech crossed on speech
Joined and secured
Now gathering speech
The rich weight glowing.

Hold now, hold,
I had to shout each time,
This that is all our doing,
This that we owe one another,
Hans, Yale, James,
Bunny in her bright tears,
Emrich, Minda Rae,
And the student always called
Sir, stray
Visitor from some

Remote class, with terms
Yet more remote, now
Held and holding
Forever with us, this
Vivid morning:
Hold, hold now
(I cry still
In a stillness)
This, such as it is,
That we have made, all of us,
And gather
With what we made.

A CHILD'S BIRTHDAY

1

A Switzerland upon
  The continent of our years
Your two years

The heap of blocks
  With burrowing trains and traffic
In the floor's traffic

Shine, a holiday
  Whose lights plunge to surprise
A child's blue lakes

Whose hours sing out from toy
  Prisons of clocks
A chorus of surprise.

2

Two years a land, its seasons
Jeweled: glacier of sun!
Held beyond holding,
Bright neutrality, free
Of the risk you are, being
What we risk, being
What we ask,

Yield only, clear
In all your lights,
Dearly this
Clearest
Diminutive
Of mountains tossed
In a fiercer love.

POEM FOR AN ANNIVERSARY

For Juliet
"... *questa cortesissima*"

Mind and ear marveled now on this language
Immediately all and nothing ever studied.
The chimes of its declensions, the courtesies poised
    in the verb,
The clear idiom though the use had faded

Would instruct the breath against the pedant's gut-
    tural
Not lost in the Song but choked on the dry claims
And against the wit constricting its own life
Open the lips and the throat to the child's exclaiming.

Over the quarreling dialects twisted on one another
And the fragments, and the syllables stunted or mute,
The pure vowel open to sweet country and sweet air
Spoke with its whole breath from past to future

And trees, stones, beasts, startling to this lexicon,
Took new being in the names they had known for-
    ever,
The old names falling away like dark encrustations.

The earth shone, as with its first rivers.

THE DISTANCES

This house, pitched now
The dark wide stretch
Of plains and ocean
To these hills over
The night-filled river,
Billows with night,
Swells with the rooms
Of sleeping children, pulls
Slowly from this bed,
Slowly returns, pulls and holds,
Is held where we
Lock all distances!

Ah, how the distances
Spiral from that
Secrecy:
Room,
Rooms, roof
Spun to the huge
Midnight, and into
The rings and rings of stars.

INSCRIPTIONS

I

A *Map Kept as a Souvenir*

The ship swallowed by time; unfriendly edges
Held by a sea horse; nothing to adorn
The vacancy but red lines of the course
Sagging from port to port. Festoons of wishes!

II

The Remembrance of a Young Girl Sketching the Children of Positano

Seeing her,
That grave child, my bride, surrounded
By the dark children clamoring to pose,
Raphaels before a pen could move, herself
Quietly and wholly of that light
Clear Botticelli,
How could I let such art upon art smile unaccounted?

And what art could I use?

III

The Letter: Morning

Her letter like a caught bird, my hand
Quieting the flutter in the wind
As now I brought it, proud, untame,
To make a bright cage of my room.

IV

The News of Winter

The thinnest word! Beware,
The empty air will say it.
Hide, or confide your heart
For this still word
To overlay it.

V

The Painting Lesson

I know on this neglected lawn
How the world knelt sweetly to be drawn.

VI

The Lovers

Under the wild moon, pressed
Against the loud earth, the lovers:
Their silence fierce as the wind,
Their pride riding the night.

VII

For a Dead Actress

Teased out of words, drawn from the dark
Of the bare stage in the dark
Theatre, where shall these phantoms rest
That served my poor phantom?

VIII

The Presence

It grows in a silence.
A silence grows from it.

IX

The Snapshot

Hazards of time
Minding no
Justice or love
In time would know
(O lovely hazard!)
Love in its justice
Just so.

PRAISE OF COMEDY: A DISCOURSE
Phi Beta Kappa Poem, College of William and Mary, 1962

My poem within a poem (for the bright riddle,
For the thread of song,
For the clear pool in a forest of disguises)
Speaks neither wisdom nor
"The love of wisdom"
But the dazzled learning
How wisdom might be loved.

The thunderous king
Commands the words to be commanded,
Orders the ordering of words
To measure love.
I praise that measure
He will traverse his kingdom
And his lost name to find
When he becomes
His Fool, gone
To bed at noon.

I praise the cage
Dreamed at last for the two birds
Where the world's gossip flows,
And one may know
A spy's pinprick
Of what God knows.
My praise is for
The measure of this knowing

48

That kneels and asks forgiveness
Answered by love
That asks a blessing.

I ask the comic muse
To light these words, granting
The self transparent with idea
In an enchantment; not
That swollen heaviness contending
Even with the stage. On either stage
The cost is a whole life: I praise
Beginning with that cost: the quick praise,
Tapers and revels
Quick with it.

So comedy, dancing, is
Dance, is
How many lights, brightening into
Pure lyric. Plato,
Writing philosophy, divined
Its muse is comic: the argument
Danced: gay dialectic! ages from
Philosophy rendered tragic, the German
Dialektik: dense
History
Quarreling into form.

I celebrate the celebration
The absent Duke
Somehow presiding: the crossed and teased
Loves learning
Behavior in that knowledge,
Brought to a sweet
Mischief in that
Benevolence.

We choose, or long to choose.
For tragedy is no choice:
It chooses us; we are already
Chosen. Only
That clearest music
Remote and immediate
Waits for consent
(Come, in your dazzle of tears!)
All else lost
In whatever is:
Voices
And civil instrument
Singing that choice.

THE PROMISING

I

Swift
Signatures of the shore:
Gulls; the thin clear
Flourish of beach;
Roofs;
Or bluff
Hieroglyphs
Striding the day;
Or white silence widening
From the silent bow—

II

Night spoke to the child.
The rain
Was words, beach
The slow word opening.
Sentence on dark
Sentence, the sea;
The shores, tracing
Shadows on stone,
Deep copper, feathered steel:
Traced
Upon tracings.

Words at the dark shore
Where the tall reeds
Bent to receive us, bent
Over again. Lights
On the lake's far side
Small dancing of blue and red
Beyond
Words' falling,
Clearest and smallest
Dream through five summers.

Sun on the wide lake
Slid to the oarlock,
Dripped, light into light;
Sun where the water
Scarcely broken
Burnished the swift
Girl's shoulder,
Flashed with the long
Sure stroke:

Dead that year,
Her sixteen years
Signed in the brightness
That summer's life
And every summer's
Word of death.

Words at the shore,
The reeds
Bent over again,

The way covered. The far shore
Phantom
With five summers.

IV

Far light, fire,
Flower of fire,
Flame, bloom:
The words become,
Worlds become.
It comes, comes:
Slow, opening
Word.

Coming that is
One's own becoming.

V

Islands waited, wait still
Where the leaves conspire
Against all words. The rain
Resolves all things to rain.
Wordless, shapeless,
The night breathes under
The words and names
And knows its own:

The smile of the mad girl
Unastonished, knowing
The visitation:
Walls
Wavering in film.

VI

"Born to say one thing,"
All the books for the one word:
The metaphor not means but end,
Not the technique
But the vocation, the destiny.
Let it be
One metaphor, deeper each time
With the life that fills it;
Let the meaning come from the abundance,
Not from the brilliance, not from some new rhetoric
Pretending to hate rhetoric
But from the overflow of meaning
Demanding even as the poem is heard
The next poem, and the next,
That are one poem.

Let it be: the poet bearing
What he was born for,
And among the words
Not meant to efface themselves in meaning,
Among the words
Wrenched into pedantry or fixed
In thin wit,
Among words traded and the small betrayals,
And there, island or city,
Where the words were all but extinguished,
Borne by that.

VII

The shore
Signs itself in silence.

If all has been for the poem
The poem has been
For the silence it comes from,
For the silence
It must create.

I have found,
Am found by
A shore of silence.

It yields these words.

It holds my word.